Japan Travel Guide

The Ultimate Japan Travel Guide for Curious, Fun, and Adventurous Travelers

TABLE OF CONTENTS

MAP 9
EPIC ITINERARY 11
NEW TO JAPAN? 15
    GETTING TO JAPAN 16
    MOVING AROUND 19
    ETIQUETTE... BE NICE CHARLIE 24
    CLIMATE 28
    GEOGRAPHY 29
    SAFETY 29
    USEFUL WEBSITES & APPS 30
HISTORY 31
JAPANESE SOCIETY TODAY 35
    BEST BOOKS & MOVIES 36
    SOCIETY, VALUES & BELIEFS 37
    POLITICS & ECONOMY 38
    RELIGION 39
    STATS 39
    FESTIVALS 39
CHARLIE'S TEN QUIRKY FACTS ABOUT JAPAN ... 43
CITY 1: TOKYO 45
CITY 2: KYOTO 57
CITY 3: OSAKA 65
CITY 4: NARA 73

3

CITY 5: OKINAWA 78
CITY 6: HOKKAIDO 84
CITY 7: HIROSHIMA 90
CHARLIE'S FAREWELL NOTE 97

JOURNEY WITH CHARLIE!

Our team's philosophy is quite simple: we travel not to escape life, but for life not to escape us.

The Unbound Charlie team understands that when we travel our senses are heightened, we question more and generally view the world as if we are children once again – completely overcome with **fun, curiosity, and adventure!**

We, the Unbound Charlie team, want you to keep that zealous spirit with the comfort of a concise and up-to-date guide! Say goodbye to the superfluous information. Say goodbye to antiquated guides. **And finally come along with Charlie for the adventure of your life!**

> "It is good to have an end to journey toward; but it is the journey that matters, in the end."
> – Ernest Hemingway

© **Copyright 2015 by Unbound Charlie Travel Co. - All rights reserved.**

This document is geared towards providing exact and reliable information in regards to the topic and issue covered. The publication is sold with the idea that the publisher is not required to render accounting, officially permitted, or otherwise, qualified services. If advice is necessary, legal or professional, a practiced individual in the profession should be ordered.

- From a Declaration of Principles which was accepted and approved equally by a Committee of the American Bar Association and a Committee of Publishers and Associations.

In no way is it legal to reproduce, duplicate, or transmit any part of this document in either electronic means or in printed format. Recording of this publication is strictly prohibited and any storage of this document is not allowed unless with written permission from the publisher. All rights reserved.

The information provided herein is stated to be truthful and consistent, in that any liability, in terms of inattention or otherwise, by any usage or abuse of any policies, processes, or directions contained within is the solitary and utter responsibility of the recipient reader. Under no circumstances will any legal responsibility or blame be held against the publisher for any reparation, damages, or monetary loss due to the information herein, either directly or indirectly.

Respective authors own all copyrights not held by the publisher.

The information herein is offered for informational purposes solely, and is universal as so. The presentation of the information is without contract or any type of guarantee assurance.

The trademarks that are used are without any consent, and the publication of the trademark is without permission or backing by the trademark owner. All trademarks and brands within this book are for clarifying purposes only and are the owned by the owners themselves, not affiliated with this document.

MAP

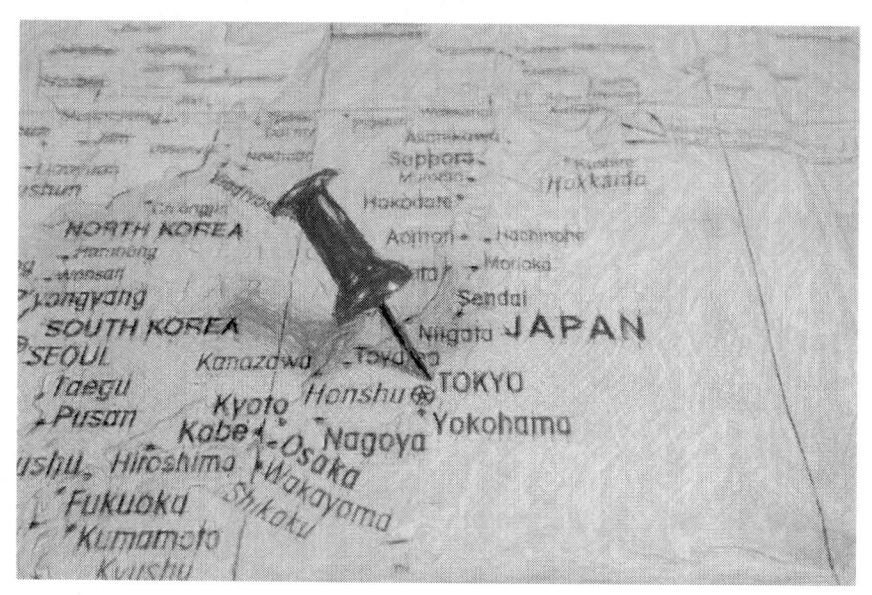

EPIC ITINERARY

Touring Japan can take months, even years to see all of the amazing temples, shrines, gardens, mountains, and other sites. A week in Tokyo may not be enough for many of you given the 20 plus city districts. The epic itinerary suggested here can be planned for 7 to 10 days, where you get to see the main sites along the Golden Route of Japan.

Day 1

Tokyo- exploring popular tourist sites like **Tokyo Tower** and the **Imperial Palace**.

Day 2

Tokyo- a side trip to Nikko to visit temples or more exploration of Tokyo museums and temples.

Day 3

Driving to **Hakone**, to enjoy the hot springs before moving on to **Kyoto** the next day. You may also want to stop at **Mount Fuji** for a short while before ending in Hakone. It will depend on how you are traveling.

Day 4 and 5

Kyoto- spend at least two days exploring the temples, gardens, and markets. **Nijo Castle**, **Kyoto Imperial Palace**, and **Sento Palace** are three highlights worth seeing. (If this is a 10-day trip, consider booking those extra 3 days in Kyoto).

Day 6

Nara is another beautiful location to visit parks, gardens, and temples, such as **Todaji Temple**, **Isuien Garden**, and **Toshodaiji Temple**.

Day 7

Osaka is famous for **Osaka Castle**. There is also the popular **Minami district**, **Osaka Aquarium**, and **Sumiyoshi Taisha** shrine.

If you have a month in Japan, you might consider traveling to all regions of Japan, starting in Tokyo, visiting Okinawa, back up the western coast to Hokkaido and returning to Tokyo to leave.

NEW TO JAPAN?

Japan is a mixture of history, culture, and respectful nature. Many of the main cities in Japan will be bustling with activity, while the countryside will have a slower pace. In tourist locations, you can expect many visitors and will need to be extremely respectful as you view the various artifacts, relics, and other items on display. You are likely to encounter a variety of dress styles from the business attire seen in major cities, to kimono wearing residents working at tourist sites or in countryside temples.

Japan has three main dialects. The standard dialect is one you may have heard before, if you watch anime or TV dramas online. The official language is called Hyojungo. The other dialects of Japan are often related to Hyojungo, where the spelling of words may vary slightly or the pronunciation is modified. Kansai dialect is spoken in western Japan mainly in the Osaka region. The third most widely spoken dialect is Tohoku, which is often associated with country folk and farmers.

Watching Japanese dramas, movies, and anime, as well as reading several books, tourist pamphlets and other materials about Japan will help lessen the unfamiliarity with a new country. Even if you have not studied the Japanese culture in depth, no worry is needed because Charlie is here to guide you in the fundamentals of traveling throughout Japan.

GETTING TO JAPAN

Flying into Japan is the most popular way of entering the country, but not the only method of entry. Almost all major airlines fly in and out of Japan, including Japan's own Japan Airlines (JAL) and All Nippon Airways (ANA). Both JAL and ANA serve international destinations. Major airports around the world provide Japan as an international destination.

Narita Airport in Tokyo is the busiest international airport in the country. Kansai Airport in Osaka is the second largest and hosts numerous international travelers each year. Haneda Airport in Tokyo and Central Japan Airport in Nagoya are the other two airports that see the heaviest traffic.

The fifth largest international airport is **Fukuoka Airport**. This airport links with several Asian locations, including

China and Korea. A few of the smaller airports also provide small international flights mainly to Korea and China.

Cruising to Japan

International travelers can also take a cruise to Japan. There are a select few transatlantic cruise ships that go to Asia. There is also a possibility of flying to Asia and taking a cruise from China, Australia, or Korea to Japan. Cruises are not as popular a method as flying into Japan due to itinerary restraints.

There are also other types of passenger ships, such as the Japan to China International Ferry Company that offers a ride between China and Japan. However, this can also eat away at the time you have allotted for your entire trip. It would make sense to take a ferry if you are already in China visiting mainland Asia and wish to extend your trip over to Japan. Ferries depart on a weekly basis.

Documentation for Travel

Entering Japan, you will need to go through Customs and state your reason for the visit. You will need a **valid passport**. The passport cannot expire before your trip to Japan is over. It is suggested that your **passport has at least six months left on the expiration date**, while traveling in Japan to avoid any validity issues. You also need to have one-page blank for the entry stamp.

A visa is not required for short-term travel (under 90 days). If you are entering the country for 91 days or more, you will need to contact your local embassy, apply and receive a visa before entering Japan. You are not allowed to work if you have entered the country without a visa. If you are visiting for work, an exchange study program, or to be with a spouse currently living in the country, you will need to have the appropriate visa.

Japan also requires "all foreign nationals entering the country to provide fingerprint scans and to be photographed at the port of entry," according to the US Government Travel Website. This is required even if the passport or visa is valid.

If you have an indirect flight taking you through a Chinese airport, you may need a Chinese visa. Consult your local embassy to determine if you need a tourist visa to change flights in China. A tourist visa is required if you are spending any time outside the airport in China before continuing to Japan.

You are not required to have any vaccinations to enter Japan for a vacation. There are no restrictions on currency for entry or exit, except to declare if you have **1,000,000 Yen** when you enter Japan.

MOVING AROUND

Japan offers several methods of transportation for local and inter-regional travel. Once you arrive at an international airport, you have the option of using any airport to book domestic, regional flights for your travel.

Rental cars are available for foreign nationals. Driving in Japan is considered expensive and complicated. Driving is done on the left side of the road and all signs are in Japanese. Highway tolls can also be extremely high. In Tokyo going 20 miles can take two hours due to traffic congestion. Japanese law also states that all drivers are liable should an accident occur. Japan has a 0 blood alcohol level for drivers and if you are pulled over for drinking, your license can be confiscated. It is better to rely on public transportation for your travel needs.

Japan offers railways, buses, taxis, ferries, and bicycles for transportation. The railway is the best way to travel around cities and other regions of Japan. Buses are best for short distance travel. Ferries are used for travel between the islands of Japan. Bicycles are also best for in city, short-distance travel.

Rail Travel

Japan has several domestic and regional trains to help you travel throughout the country. If you are traveling a long distance and wish to do so in the shortest amount of time the **Shinkasen** is the best option. It is the bullet train or a high-speed train. There are also night trains, with sleeper compartments for traveling 24 hours a day.

The **Seishun 18 Kippu** is a cheap ticket offering unlimited travel on local trains. However, it is valid for rides within a 5-day period. It is a season pass, meaning it is only available at certain times of the year. This is an option if your itinerary is set in one city, such as Tokyo. The current price is **11,850 Yen**.

For unlimited, nationwide travel the **Japan Rail Pass** is best. This pass will help you move from region to region. The Japan Rail Pass (JR Pass) must be purchased before you arrive in Japan. It is only available through your home country. When you arrive, you provide a voucher to the railway, and the railway then gives you the JR Pass. The reason for limiting the purchase outside of Japan is because it is not available to Japanese residents. You can purchase the JR Pass for 7, 14, or 21 days, meaning during this period of time you can ride the trains without paying for a new pass. It must also be consecutive days. It works on all JR trains, including the bullet trains, local trains, limited express trains, and some JR Buses. The pass can also work on the JR Ferry to Miyajima. The prices are as follows:

- **29,110 Yen for 7 days**
- **46,390 Yen for 14 days**
- **59,350 Yen for 21 days**

There are other passes available specific to the region you may be traveling to, such as Hokkaido, Japan East, Tokyo specific, Nikko, Fujisawa, Kamakura, Hakone, Fuji, and Ito. Kansai rail passes are also available. However, if you are visiting various areas of Japan, the JR rail pass will still be the best option because it works on all JR trains, nationwide.

Buses

The JR rail pass will work on the JR buses. For local, short distance travel, you will discover Tokyo, Osaka and most large cities will have a bus. The system is designed to complement trains and subway networks. In places like Kyoto, where train networks are not as prolific, the bus system is the best means of public transportation. Buses will serve the smaller towns, national parks, and countryside. There are also major cities linked by highway and long distance buses.

Unlike the US and many other countries, you will enter the bus through the back door, pick up a ticket, and later use that ticket to determine your fare. If you planned ahead and bought an IC card, you can touch the card to the sensor. An IC card is the simplest method, as you will not have to calculate the rate based on the display above the driver, which shows the next stop and the fares for that stop. When your stop is approaching, press one of the buttons on the wall of the bus to let the driver know you want to get off. There is a change machine that you can use to get the exact fare. Some locations like Kyoto have a flat fare for all stops.

Buses in Tokyo are also an exception. You enter through the front and exit through the rear, with a flat fare to go around the city.

Note: IC cards are interchangeable cards that can be used to make payments on public transportation, vending machines, restaurants, and shops. You load the card with Yen at bus depots, subways, and train stations and then use it as needed. However, the IC card is not available in all areas and you cannot travel outside or between IC card areas. It is best if you intend on staying in one city, visiting nearby national parks and tourist's stops, versus region-to-region traveling.

Long distance, highway buses offer a more affordable option than express trains. Some trains do have overnight travel. The Willer Express is the cheaper option for interregional travel and it is one of the few systems to have English operators.

JR Buses are more expensive, but are definitely cheaper than the trains. For JR pass use, the Nohi, Fujikyu, Keio, Meitetsu, and Alpico buses are available and ones with English operators.

Bus tickets can be purchased at major terminals, by phone, convenience stores, or through travel agents. You can also purchase tickets online. Seat reservations are provided for long, overnight travel.

Since the fares do change based on destination, length of the ride, and interregional travel, it is difficult to list the specific fare. However, the cost for a bus trip in the city is lower than a taxi and interregional travel is less expensive than the trains.

Taxi Services

Taxi services in large services are highly expensive compared to buses. Buses and trains will stop at midnight, so plan on using a taxi if you are out late at a club, dinner, or other vacation activity. Be prepared for long lines for taxis on Friday and Saturday nights. In the smaller cities, Kyoto, and the countryside, taking a taxi from the train station is a good alternative for reaching your destination.

Taxis in Japan are quite trustworthy and do not attempt to take advantage of clients, in most cases. A green license plate indicates a licensed taxi. A white and yellow license plate is for regular cars. Fare calculation will be by the meter, unless on a popular tourist route, such as an airport to hotel route, which may have a flat rate.

The fares can also differ a little based on region, the size of the vehicle, and the company providing the service. **Typically, a four passenger taxi will be 600 to 700 Yen for the first two kilometers and about 80 to 90 Yen for each additional 300 to 400 meters traveled.**

Evening rates, particularly during rush hour, will mean an increase of approximately 20 percent of the fare. If there are expressway tolls these add to the fare.

ETIQUETTE... BE NICE CHARLIE

Etiquette is very important to the Japanese. As a foreigner traveling in Japan, it is paramount that you have a general understanding of greetings, table manners, tipping, physical contact, attire, and other etiquette rules. There are rules for how to behave inside the house/hotel, shrines/temples, for bathing, toileting needs, dining, sitting, and greeting.

Greetings

Bowing, in Japan, is how people greet each other. For visitors, you will be expected to **nod your head in greeting**. A deeper, longer bow is one of respect, while a nod is informal. A bow with hands is not necessary, unlike other Asian cultures. If you have a formal meeting while in Japan, an exchange of business cards, along with the deeper bow is expected. At most shops and restaurants, you will be greeted with a formal bow, but you can nod in reciprocation.

Table Manners

Japan normally has lower tables, with cushions on a tatami floor; however, in most restaurants you will see western style chairs. If you eat in a restaurant that has a tatami floor, you will be expected to remove your shoes or slippers before stepping in. You also need to avoid stepping on any other cushion in the room.

When eating, you will be provided with wet towels, at most restaurants, to wash your hands before the meal. When your order is served, it is a sign of respect to say "**Itadakimasu**," which means, "**I gratefully receive**" this meal. If others at the table are still awaiting their meal you may hear "osaki ni dozo" meaning to please go ahead and eat. You can also say "osaki ni itadakimasu" meaning "allow me to start before you."

Small bowls are meant to be picked up, lifted to your mouth and drank from. Larger dishes are meant to be eaten with chopsticks. Some western style restaurants or tourist locations will provide utensils.

Burping, audible eating, and blowing your nose at the table are all considered bad manners. You are also supposed to eat all items served; with not a single grain of rice left or you will insult the restaurant and/or server.

After a meal, it is good manners to set your dishes how they were when they were served, meaning in the same place with the chopsticks on your napkin or resting on the chopstick rest. Also say "**gochisosama deshita**" at the end. It means "thank you for the feast."

Drinking is usually done once everyone has his or her glass. If you are hosting the meal, you serve everyone, and salute with the word "**Kampai**" before everyone takes a drink.

Tipping

Depending on where you go, you may be expected to tip in Japan. For example, some of the more tourist restaurants will add 10% to your bill for large parties. However, if you are going around on your own, without a tour group, then tipping is not necessary. Customarily, in Japan servers and other workers feel it is rude to tip for good service, because providing excellent service is standard, not something to be tipped extra for. If you do feel a tip is necessary at your accommodation, for a tour guide at a museum, or in any other situation, you must place the tip in an envelope. Never try to directly hand cash to anyone, as this will offend them.

Physical Contact

Many Asian countries, including Japan are less inclined to accept physical contact, particularly from strangers. Shaking hands is acceptable, only because it is a known western greeting. However, hugs, kissing as a greeting, and backslapping to show happiness are not acceptable. You can hold hands in public with your family or friends; however, PDA are less acceptable unless in a hostess or host bar.

Attire

Your attire should be clean, without holes or stains. Otherwise, anything is acceptable. You will notice in some areas there are Japanese walking around in Cosplay costumes as a normal part of their day. Japan is understanding of the western culture and their dressing style. In saying that, you should respect their customs and culture, particularly in the temples. Wearing a few nice outfits when visiting shrines and temples is better than going in wearing short shorts and tank tops. You also want to have easy to remove shoes simply because entering certain locations like shrines and temples require the removal of your shoes.

Other Etiquette Suggestions

When visiting shrines and temples, it is customary to offer a prayer in front of sacred objects. If you do not know what to do or are not religious, simply be calm and respectful of those around you. Go at a slow pace, based on those around you. In many of the temples you will need to remove your shoes, place them on the shelves at the entrance or use the plastic bags when provided. Always, always have socks with you. They should be nice, without dirt or holes. The best thing you can do is not draw attention to yourself in any situation, as this is the best sign of respect.

CLIMATE

Japan has snow, rain, cold seasons, and warm summer months. In winter, expect dry and sunny days along the Pacific coast, with temperatures above 32 degrees F. Southern Japan is more temperate, with mild winters. Summer will have a monsoon season between June and July, with temperatures in the 90s. Summer usually ends in August. Spring is from March to May with temperatures that are comfortable, but not overly hot. Autumn, which lasts from September to November will have light breezes and temperatures of 46 to 55 degrees F. Spring is considered the best time to travel, given the favorable temperatures and less rainfall.

GEOGRAPHY

Japan is made up of a series of islands and over 200 volcanoes. The coastal regions have beaches, sea level heights, and as you go west or east from the coast, you will see more mountains and higher elevations. Kyoto and Osaka are inland; therefore, they have more hills and mountains.

SAFETY

As with any country, you do need to be prepared for emergencies and understand how to remain safe on holiday. Japan is known for its earthquakes, with many small, barely felt earthquakes throughout the year. Always be aware of your surroundings, avoid areas that are less reputable, and know how to contact local agencies such as police, ambulance and tourist police. Have the following numbers with you just in case:

POLICE: 119

AMBULANCE: 119

TOURIST POLICE: 110

US EMBASSY: 03-3224-5000 or 03-6743-9732

USEFUL WEBSITES & APPS

- US Embassy: Japan.usembassy.gov
- Japan-Guide.com
- Hostelworld.com: hotels and hostels
- JNTO- us.jnto.go.jp- official tourism guide for Japan
- Fodors.com for language and activities
- www.tofugu.com- for common phrases to use on vacation

Apps

- JR Pass app for train information
- Maps with Me
- Navitime
- Imiwa
- Yomiwa
- Line, Skype, or other similar apps
- GuruNavi
- NHK World Radio

HISTORY

Japan is not just a country founded on the Shogun and Samurai, although both are a very important part of the country's history. Japan is believed to have formed prior to the Paleolithic time period, around 30,000 BC. The island mass formed through volcanic activity, some of which are still ongoing today. Like many countries, there were early hunter-gatherer cultures, who are thought to be the ancestors of the Ainu and Yamato people. By 300 BC, Japan was bustling with intermingled cultures, including the Yayoi people who traveled from the mainland and began teaching new practices to the Jomon people. In 500 BC, the Yayoi period began, where wet-rice farming, new pottery styles, and metallurgy were introduced from Korea and China. It was in the third century BC, that Japan's written history appeared in the Chinese Book of Han, recording the Three Kingdoms of Japan. It was also during this time that

Buddhism was introduced and was widely accepted during the **Asuka Period**, which lasted from 592 to 710.

Following the Asuka period was the **Nara period**, which was short lived (710 to 784). The imperial court resided in Heijo-kyo or modern day Nara. It was a time of Buddhist development and also sickness, with smallpox taking nearly one-third of the population. The **Heian period** began next, lasting until 1185. It was a time of great cultural advancement, particularly in art, prose, and poetry.

The feudal era is perhaps the period many of us remember best. It was the emergence of the **samurai** and ruling shogunates. The Taira clan during the Genpei War was an epic tale in which **Minamoto no Yoritomo** was appointed **shogun** and established the Kamakura period, lasting until 1333. The samurai repelled Mongol invasions until 1281, when Emperor Go-Daigo overthrew the ruling shogun. In 1336, Ashikaga Takauji defeated Go-Daigo and established himself as the shogunate in Muromachi, Kyoto. This was a prosperous age for the Ashikaga shogunates and led to the evolution of the Higashyama Culture. This era of Ashikaga rule lasted until the 16th century, but was not without its turmoil, such as the Sengoku Period or Warring States time.

By the 15th century, Jesuit missionaries arriving from Portugal reached the country, providing cultural and commercial exchange between Japan and the West. Oda Nobunaga rose to power collecting firearms and technology, which he used to conquer the individual states in Japan. This period was known as the Azuchi - Momoyama, lasting from

1573 to 1603. On a trip to Japan, particularly in the Kyoto region, you are likely to see historical accounts of **Oda Nobunaga** and the **Azuchi-Momoyama period**.

Toyotomi Hideyoshi came to power after Nobunaga was assassinated. He attempted twice to invade Korea. It was in the 1600s, that **Tokugawa Ieyasu** served as regent and he would eventually name himself emperor and move the capital to **Edo**, modern Tokyo. The Tokugawa shogunate closed Japan, isolating it for two and a half centuries from western influences. It was also a time that game rise to national studies.

Japan had to battle with Korea and China to maintain power of their island chain throughout its history. More than once, Japan also fought for the rights to own Jeju Island, which is still a bone of contention between Korea (who holds ownership) and Japan, who felt the island should be theirs based on the long string of islands making up the country.

The modern era of Japan started with **Commodore Matthew Perry** and the **Black Ships** of the US Navy. Arriving in Japan on March 31, 1854, he forced the **Convention of Kanagawa** and opened trade to Japan. The **Boshin War** led to a centralized state, with a unified Japan under the Emperor, which also began the **Meiji Restoration** period.

Japan began making advancements towards military power, establishing a Cabinet, the Privy Council, and the Imperial Diet. In 1884 to 1885 and 1904 to 1905, there was the **First**

Sino-Japanese War and **Russo-Japanese War**, respectively. Both helped Japan gain control of Korea, Taiwan, and the southern section of Sakhalin. During the First World War, Japan increased its territorial holdings, and rule of Korea, as well as occupying Manchuria. A **Second Sino-Japanese War** in 1937 to 1945, allowed Japan to invade China and capture **Nanjing**. This also led to the involvement of Japan in the Second World War and the subsequent attacks on Pearl Harbor. A new constitution was started in 1947 to bring more liberal democratic practices to the political forefront, enabling Japan to be granted membership in the United Nations in 1956. Japan focused more on internal growth for the economy, eventually becoming second in the world with regards to economic size.

JAPANESE SOCIETY TODAY

Japan's society today has changed little in some ways and a great deal in others. There is still a very homogeneous society, with 1% of the population made up of Koreans and Chinese. Many customs have carried over from era to era with regards to respect and understanding. Shinto and Buddhism are the main religions, although Christianity and Confucianism remain. Where society has improved is the ability to have more individualism than in prior eras. During the shogun and Samurai eras, women helped in the fields, raising children, and running the household, while the men learned to be great warriors. Suicide was expected for failure and perfectly acceptable, even demanded in certain situations. This has changed little, although less used as a means of keeping the family honor.

Today, there is nothing surprising in walking in places like Harajuku and finding Cosplayers. Dressing to show fandom of a favorite anime is normal for teens when out with friends. Yet, in serious settings such as school, children must wear uniforms and not stand out among their peers, except for academic excellence. Bullying, which is often seen in Japanese teen dramas is a very real problem, not something created for entertainment. Going to school in Japan can lead to great bullying, where the teachers have more control than parents. Sometimes teachers will go to the homes of students to bring them to school, to talk with the parents, and to address issues. Teachers are considered a secondary part of the family.

BEST BOOKS & MOVIES

One of the best ways to learn about the Japanese culture and society is to watch Japanese Dramas, which have been subtitled like **Beautiful Rain**; **Rich Man, Poor Woman**; and **Yae's Sakura**.

American based films such as **The Last Samurai** and **Black Rain** are also worth watching. The Last Samurai offers a look at the Nobunaga period, when firearms were being brought into Japan and it was nearing the end of the samurai way of life. Black Rain takes a more modern approach to depict the Yakuza, as well as the society, albeit fictionalized, to show the hierarchy and respect required of a Japanese resident.

For books, consider reading **The Chrysanthemum and the Sword**, which shows a postwar Japanese culture. Princess Masako offers a controversial look at the Imperial Family, but valuable for educational purposes. **Hitching Rides with Buddha** or **Hokkaido Highway Blues** by Will Ferguson is an account of a visitor who toured Japan. It offers great insight into modern Japan, with cultural distinctions based on real interactions.

SOCIETY, VALUES & BELIEFS

Values are a great part of everyday life in Japan. Their etiquette rules are to be followed, arguments are uncommon between parents and children, and disrespect is considered a great offense. Japan is also a very orderly, empathetic country. There is social order, where status is clearly defined by the language for age and gender.

Respect must always be given to those who are older or have seniority in the family, education, and employment sphere. The language is designed to show superiority and inferiority, with regards to the hierarchy.

In modern eras, there is less focus on religion, but this does not mean beliefs are not important with regards to ancestral rites.

POLITICS & ECONOMY

Japan is ruled by a Liberal Democratic Party. It is still a constitutional monarchy, which uses a parliamentary cabinet system to make new laws. There is a prime minister and 17 ministers of state that make up the "Diet" or cabinet. The prime minister is a member of the House of Representatives and has the power to appoint or remove ministers of state. The constitution began in 1947 and has 103 articles.

Today, Japan's economy is the third largest in the world, with the fourth largest purchasing power parity. It is considered the second largest developed economy. Japan has maintained a proper balance, rather than a government deficit due to the exportation of many goods. However, the

2010 recession and 2011 earthquake greatly shook the nation's stability, allowing China to become the second largest economy in terms of GDP.

RELIGION

Japanese residents will follow Shinto, Buddhism, Confucianism, or Christianity. However, it is not a big part of everyday life. During festivals, weddings, and funerals are when religion plays a larger part in a person's life.

STATS

POPULATION: 127.1 Million
GDP: $4.8 trillion, with -0.1% growth
UNEMPLOYMENT RATE: 3.7%
BELIEF SYSTEM: Shinto is still the main religion of Japan at about 51%, and Buddhism is a close second at 34%.
DEMOGRAPHY BREAKDOWN: Japanese make up 98.5% of the population, with Koreans 0.05%, Chinese 0.04% and other listed as 0.06%, mainly Brazil, Peru, and Filipino. The highest populations are in large cities like Tokyo. The population also consists mainly of children 0-14 and adults 55-64, with the highest population percentage of people 65 years and older. There have been low birth rates in the last decade.

FESTIVALS

Japan has numerous festivals throughout the year that are regionally specific. Many of these festivals are associated with shrines; however, there are top national festivals that you may wish to see while traveling around Japan. These festivals relate to national holidays, where most of the time specific traditions or groups of people are celebrated.

The most famous festival is **Golden Week**. This national holiday lasts for a week and usually starts the last week of April, on Emperor Showa's birthday. The week is filled with holidays including **Greenery Day, Showa Day, Constitution Memorial Day, Citizen's Holiday, and Children's Day**. Golden Week was named in 1948, when the National Holiday Laws declared 9 total holidays as official. Since these holidays were already at the end of April and in early May, it was decided that the week should be named based on radio lingo, which is "golden time" and the highest ratings for listeners.
For Japanese, many take the week as their vacation time and some companies completely close allowing their employees time off.

Japanese New Year

Like many countries, January 1st is celebrated as the New Year. It is celebrated as a holiday, where businesses will close, most often through January 3rd. Fireworks in large cities are part of the celebration as Japan brings in a new year. **Bonenkai Parties** or **Year Forgetting Parties** are held to celebrate the end of the year and that old worries and troubles need to be left behind. On New Year's Eve tradition states toshikoshi soba should be served to symbolize longevity. In recent years a music show, **Kohaku Uta Gassen**, is on television with many Enka singers and J-pop performances. Traditional Japanese will celebrate by viewing the first sunrise of the new year and then visiting a shrine or temple.

Seijin no Hi or **Coming of Age** is a national festival for 20 year olds to celebrate their life. In Japan, drinking, smoking and voting is allowed only when a person reaches 20. The holiday is celebrated on January 15. For visitors, it can be fun to take part in celebrating their life.

National Foundation Day

Kenkoku Kinenbi or National Foundation Day is a national celebration of the first Japanese emperor. The history books recorded the first crowning of the first emperor as 660 BC. The holiday is February 11.

Valentine's Day

It is not considered a national holiday; however, it is often celebrated. However, in Japan women will either buy or make chocolates to give to men to show their love or to ask a guy out. It is the opposite for most cultures, where men are supposed to treat a woman and show their love. For the men, they can still do this on a specific day, called White Day. It is a month after valentine's day, where the men return gifts to women if they appreciated the woman's gesture.

Other national holidays, which have festival activities include the Spring Equinox, Ocean Day, Mountain Day, and Respect for the Aged Day. Many of the national holidays pay respect to the departed or to specific age groups. Bunka no Hi is another very important holiday, which translates as Culture Day. Culture Day is meant to promote the love of peace and freedom. Schools and governments award specific people for special cultural achievements.

There is also a national holiday festival to celebrate the current emperor. The day will change with the new emperor; however, currently the date is December 23.

CHARLIE'S TEN QUIRKY FACTS ABOUT JAPAN

1. Christmas is celebrated more like Valentine's Day or as a lover's holiday, than the Christian concept.

2. 70% of Japan is mountainous, with over 200 volcanoes.

3. Detective Conan is the longest running Anime and Manga, and helped inspire the Anime culture in the US.

4. Musk Melon is like cantaloupe, a rare delicacy that is usually sold for over $300 USD.

5. Japan has four writing systems: Romaji, Hiragana, Kanji, and Katakana.

6. About 85% of Jamaica's coffee production is imported to Japan.

7. Japan has a nearly 100% literacy rate.

8. Japan's toilets are mostly a built in bidet and toilet combination; however, the traditional Japanese floor toilet is found in public restrooms.

9. Baseball is a close second in sports, against the National Sport Sumo wrestling.

10. The first Japanese Novel was written by Murasaki Shikibu in 1007. She was a Japanese noblewoman and titled the book The Tale of Genji.

CITY 1: TOKYO

CHARLIE'S QUICK INTRO AND HISTORY

Tokyo was formerly Edo. During the 16th century until 1868, Edo was a political center. Takugawa Ieyasu established his government in the city and eventually it grew into one of the most populated areas. The Meiji Restoration in 1868, changed the capital from Kyoto to Edo and the emperor renamed the city to mean "Eastern Capital." A major part of Tokyo was damaged in the 1923 Great Kanto Earthquake and the 1945 air raids. Today, Tokyo is a bustling metropolis and the capital of Japan. It is one of 47 prefectures, with 23 central city wards and cities, towns, and villages, which are west of the city center. Ogasawara and Izu Islands are considered part of Tokyo.

Visitors can enjoy unlimited shopping, culture, entertainment, and dining. Asakusa is one district that is filled with history, including historic temples, gardens and museums. Tokyo also has several green spaces for the health of the city residents.

CHARLIE'S FAVORITE TOUR SIGHTS & ADVENTURES

> Tokyo is a city full of cultural, historical sites, museums, urban, outdoor, and nature adventures. Discover some of the most popular tour sights.

Sights Categories: Cultural, Historical Sites, Museums

- **Tsukiji Fish Market**: this is Japan's largest and busiest market for fish. The fish market handles over 2,000 tons of various marine products each day. The bustling sellers, buyers, scooters, and trucks continue to make this a tourist spot for seeing every day culture in Japan.
- **Tokyo Imperial Palace**: the palace is located at the former Edo Castle location. It is close to Tokyo station and also the current residence of the Imperial Family. The palace was rebuilt after World War II, due to damage to the original palace. There is a large plaza, where visitors are able to view the Nijubashi. The Nijubashi is a double bridge that marks the entrance to the inner palace grounds.
- **Yasukuni Shrine**: one of the many shrines in the city, but specifically dedicated to the deities of Japan's fallen in wars.
- **Ginza**: it is actually a district within Tokyo, but worth a half-day or full day of exploration. It is the premier shopping district and one that will provide the current Japanese culture.
- **Kanda** is another district in Tokyo. It is northeast of the palace. While not a prime tourist location, it has several important sites like the **Confucian School**, **Ochanomizu Musical Instrument Area** and **Akihabara**, which is an anime mecca. Kanda Myojun Shrine often brings tourists who want to see as many shrines as possible on their trip to Japan.
- **Tokyo National Museum**: this is one of the oldest Japanese museums and highly rated by visitors. The museum was established in the Yushima Seido Shrine

in 1972, before being moved to Ueno Park. The museum contains more than 110,000 items, and close to 100 national treasures. The permanent display contains approximately 4,000 items. The museum is spread out over six buildings.

- **Edo-Tokyo Museum** is another superb location for learning about the history and early culture of Japan. The museum offers interactive exhibits to show the way of life, Edo architecture, and cultural heritage that shaped Japan.
- **Ryogoku** is the center for Sumo Wrestling and worth a look if you enjoy the national sport of Japan.
- **Harajuku** is the location for teen fashion and Cosplay.

Adventure Categories: Urban, Outdoors, & Nature Activities

- **Koishikawa Korakuen** is a landscaped garden near the Tokyo Dome.
- **Imperial East Gardens** can be enjoyed while on the Imperial Palace Grounds.
- **Hama Rikyu** is a landscaped garden, with a bike path for those who want a little exercise to see the urban areas contained within the major metropolis.
- **Rikugien** is a Japanese landscape garden, with interesting bridges, cherry blossoms, and other native plants.
- **Botanical Garden at the University of Tokyo** is yet another outdoor location to enjoy.

- **Tokyo Tower** is 333 meters tall and the symbol of the city. It is definitely the center of the urban expanse.
- **Tokyo Water Bus** provides a different view of the urban landscape.
- **Tokyo Disney Sea** is a theme park and the only one in the world that is based on nature activities.
- **Fuji Five Lakes** is a nature activity outside of Tokyo, where visitors can view Mount Fuji and enjoy the lakes surrounding the base of the mountain.

SHOPPING

1. **Shinjuku** is one of the biggest entertainment and shopping districts within Tokyo. It is close to major transportation, including buses and trains. Approximately a dozen major Japanese department stores and outlets are found in this district. Many of the largest electronics retailers can be found in this area.
2. **Shibuya** is a youth fashion, shopping district. This is where many of the teen fashions are created. Dozens of small boutiques with designer brands are found in this area. It is also considered a very vibrant area compared to Aoyama and Daikanyama.
3. **Harajuku** is a mixture of high fashion and counter culture. Several unique boutiques, designer shops, and cafes dot the street in this district.
4. **Odaiba** is located on the manmade island in Tokyo Bay. It is a trendy mall with Aquacity, Diver City, and Decks shopping malls. Palette Town is Venice themed.

5. **Tokyo Solmachi** is located at the base of Tokyo Skytree. Over 300 shops and restaurants are located at this location.

FESTIVALS

Tokyo has several important festivals relating to Golden Week, as well as city versus national festivals. **Sanja Festival**, for example, is located in Asakusa. It is a three-day festival held at Sensoji Temple. Food stalls, revelers, festival games, and Japanese drums and flutes add to the ambiance. Kanda Matsuri or Festival is one of three famous festivals, the others being Sanno Matsuri and the aforementioned Sanja. A daylong procession through central Tokyo is the highlight of this celebration. It is one that dates back to the Edo Period and the Tokugawa Shogun. Sanno Festival is a week long, with a parade going through central Tokyo. The parade ends at Hie Shrine, which enshrines the Tokyo guardian deity. It honors the gods that keep the city safe.

RESTAURANTS... CHARLIE'S CHOW TIME

Cuisine is very important to Tokyoites. Numerous districts have streets filled with one restaurant after another serving popular dishes like ramen, soba, yakitori, and kushiyaki. These districts can be considered budget, versus the fine dining that will often greet you around some of the premier tourist locations.

BUDGET

- **Midori Zushi** or Mawashi-Zushi Katsu is a popular conveyor-belt sushi restaurant -it is operated by the large chain Midori Zushi, which might account for its reasonable prices. For **100 Yen to 500 Yen** you can get over 200 kinds of dishes, many of which are sushi and side dishes. A popular new dish is their Sushi and Cheese, made with Parmesan.
- **Eichan** is part of the Kushikatsu chain based out of Osaka. The chain and particularly Eichan is known for their deep fried skewers, which can contain fish, chicken, or other ingredients. They also serve Oden for **100 Yen**. The lunch menu offers many items for **500 Yen**. There is also a seat charge at night of **200 Yen**.
- **Harajuku Gyoza Lou** is a specialty location for Chinese dumplings or Gyoza. The menu offers 6 pieces of boiled or fried gyoza for **290 Yen**. You can get the dumplings with or without garlic. They have a few simple side dishes. A full meal is usually less than **1,000 Yen**.
- For those who are not a fan of sushi and in dire need of a western meal there is BERG. They serve coffee, ham, bread, and sausages, with most menu items and drinks priced at **500 Yen**. This is one restaurant where smoking is not prohibited.

FANCY

The fancy restaurants mentioned here are all Michelin-starred. They are relatively affordable; however, for most of them you will need to make a reservation.

- **Ginza Kojyu** is a comfortable restaurant, where you can watch your meal be prepared. Sashimi and the vegetable side dishes are their most exceptional dish. Lunch is **21,600 Yen** and Dinner is **27,000 Yen**, with the tax included. It is for the Chef's Choice Course. Other items are similar in cost.
- **Ishikawa** offers another intimate dining experience, with personal staff attending the table and a prep table in front of the guests. There are several fixed courses that include an appetizer, soup, grilled main, and sashimi. The servers are kimono-clad to offer a bit of history. The restaurant is only open for dinner, prices begin at **19,000 Yen**, and reservations are required. Also young children 12 years or younger are not permitted.
- **Joel Robuchon** is a well-known restaurant offering French cuisine. There are several fixed menus, as well as a few a la carte items. The restaurant is known for its desert of Kyoho grape mocha with almond ice cream, honey coulis, and soya milk. Menu items start at **10,000 Yen** and increase based on time of day and fixed price item.
- **Narisawa** is named for Chef Yoshihiro Narisawa who spent time in France, Italy, and Switzerland perfecting his techniques. The restaurant is known for Bread of the Forest and Moss Butter. There are a lunch and dinner course, which are fixed price at **20,000 and 25,000 Yen**, respectively.

NIGHTLIFE & ENTERTAINMENT... CHARLIE'S PARTY TIME

There are plenty of places in Tokyo to view the bright city lights such as the **Tokyo Skytree**, **Tokyo Tower**, and **Tokyo Metropolitan Government Building**. Several also have top floor restaurants. However, if you like clubs, bars, and the party life you will need to go to Shinjuku, Ginza, or Shibuya districts. Roppongi is also a suggestion, but mostly filled with hostess clubs and military laden bars. Shibuya is more for the younger generations, while Ginza offers more upscale bars and nightclubs. Ginza is akin to LA or NYC prices for clubs and unless you know Japanese, you may find it difficult to get in. Another option is to take walks in Sensoji at Asakusa. The temple grounds are open for night strolls.

LODGING... CHARLIE CHILL TIME

Tokyo has domestic hotel chains, dormitories, hostels, capsule hotels, and Ryokan. Ryokan are like bed and breakfast guesthouses, often with more traditional Japanese customs.

BUDGET

Backpackers Hotel K's House Tokyo was opened in 2006 to be a clean, inexpensive location, just a minute from Kuramae station. It is in Asakusa and only 10 minutes from premium sightseeing locations. They have an English staff, free Wi-Fi, and no curfew. Rates are around **4,550 Yen** per night, but it depends on the season.

Imano Tokyo Hostel is another budget friendly location for **5,347 Yen** and up per night. They offer free Wi-Fi, a bunk with private curtain, and reading light.

Khaosan Tokyo Kabuki is a family friendly hostel, with private shower and bathrooms in the rooms. It is a better choice for those looking for cheap, but private rooms. The rates are from **3,900 Yen** a night.

FANCY

Park Hyatt Tokyo Hotel: a world-renowned hotel chain, it is 15 minutes from Shinjuku Station. It was featured in Lost in Translation. Rates are quite high and will vary based on the season, but expect **72,900 Yen** and up for a two night, three-day stay.

The Keio Plaza Hotel is a four-star hotel in the Shinjuku District. It is also a recently renovated hotel, among the many in the area. The area is known for its towering buildings and for its hotel chains. The hotel will offer every amenity you could desire including an outdoor pool and a separate pool for kids. Rates vary from **22,700 Yen** a night and up.

HIDDEN GEMS... CHARLIE'S TOP NON-TOURIST SITES

Often in favor of Disney theme parks, tourists do not consider Hanayashiki. It is located in a small corner of Asakusa. It was opened in 1853 mostly as a scenic garden, but quickly turned into an amusement park, with 22 attractions and rides. It has Japan's oldest roller coaster, ninja and kimono demonstrations, daily music performances, and a Japanese-horror haunted house.

Science and biology buffs will love the Meguro Parasitological Museum. It was started in 1953 and contains over 60,000 specimens. About 300 are on display at any given time. It might sound like a gross concept, but it is highly educational for those who love science.

Robot Restaurant is another interesting, non-tourist location. It offers a cabaret show that is more like an action video game. LED lights, techno music, Taiko drumming, and an hour show later and you will see why it can be a great laugh to visit this location.

CITY 2: KYOTO

CHARLIE'S QUICK INTRO AND HISTORY

Kyoto was the capital of Japan for more than 1,000 years, leaving it as a city and prefecture of Japan that is filled with history, culture, and beauty. Kyoto draws in the same or even slightly more tourists each year than Tokyo due to its varied past. As an ancient capital, some of the structures have not survived due to fires and wars. Thankfully, Kyoto's historic value saved it from the atomic bomb and air raids. This has left a few of the ancient buildings, as well as some recreated structures for visitors to enjoy. Kyoto is also home to several modern technological industries. Countless festivals and religious Shinto rituals are held in Kyoto, such as the Gion Matsuri. Be prepared to enjoy natural beauty, arts, and culinary culture, while visiting this prefecture and city.

CHARLIE'S FAVORITE TOUR SIGHTS & ADVENTURES

Kyoto's rein as the capital city has left it a place for cultural abundance, but it is not to be outdone in nature activities either.

Sights Categories: Cultural, Historical Sites, Museums

1. Niji Castle: this castle is historically significant to Tokugawa Ieyasu and his grandson. It is divided into three areas based on defense and an internal garden worth seeing.

2. Kyoto Imperial Palace: this was the residence of the imperial family until 1868, when the capital was moved to Tokyo permanently.
3. Sento Palace: Sento Imperial Palace is a secondary palace to the main Imperial Palace, and across from the Kyoto Imperial Palace and Park. It was built in 1630, but the original structure burned down in 1854. When the current Prince and Princess visit Kyoto they use this palace.
4. Kyoto Manga Museum: this is an international manga museum built in 2006 to show the largest collection of manga both domestic and international. Many of the exhibits are translated for all visitors.
5. Honganji Temples: Nishi Honganji and Higashi Honganji are two temples in the center of Kyoto, and rather large. They are the headquarters for the Jodo-Shin Sect, the largest Buddhist sect in Japan. Nishi Honganji is a Unesco World Heritage site. It dates back to 1591. Higashi Honganji was built 11 years later.

Adventure Categories: Urban, Outdoors, & Nature Activities

1. Kyoto Aquarium: The Kyoto aquarium is a fun, scientific activity and considered one of Japan's top aquariums. It is designed to reflect Kyoto's aquatic life, as well as show world zones like Antarctica.
2. Kyoto Tower: close to Kyoto Station, Kyoto Tower is the tallest Urban landmark in the city standing 131

meters in height. It was built in 1964 and offers views of the entire city, as well as Osaka on a good day.
3. Kyoto Station: an urban wonder, Kyoto Station was constructed on the 1200th anniversary of the former capital. It offers a futuristic design by Hara Hiroshi and yet maintains a semblance of historical Kyoto.
4. Philosopher's Path: a stone path built in the northern section of Kyoto; it lines a canal and has hundreds of cherry trees. The path was named after Nishida Kitaro, a most prominent philosopher in Japanese history.
5. Maruyama Park: a public park, adjacent to Yasaka Shrine and perfect for seeing the April cherry blossoms. The main highlight is shidarezakura or the weeping cherry tree.

SHOPPING

1. Sanjo-Dori Street: this is a street shopping mall, located near Sanjo Bridge. It is mainly a shopping area for younger generations.
2. Shinkyogoku-Dori Street: is considered a mecca for student travelers, who wish to find gift shops and department stores.
3. Shijo-Dori: is a main street of Kyoto, where the Haneikai Shopping Street is located. Surrounded by many temples this location has plenty of gift shops and tourist locations. There is also Nishiki Market, which is known as "Kyoto's Kitchen" due to the numerous food locations. Crafts are often seen here, as well as, clothing shops for day-to-day fashions.

4. The JR Kyoto Station is considered the second largest mall/shopping area with big retailers like BIC Camera electronics and "The Cube."
5. Flea markets are popular in Kyoto for tourists like the one held on the 25th of every month at Kitano Tenmangu Shrine.

FESTIVALS

Kyoto has numerous shrines that host festivals throughout the year. A few of the more well-known festivals are Gion, Aoi, Kidai, and Hanatoro. Hanatoro is an illumination event that occurs in March. It is to represent the flower and light road, where thousands of lanterns are light and let go to traverse the sky.

Gion Masturi is held at Yasaka Shrine and perhaps the most famous of Japanese festivals. It is held for an entire month in July. Several events, including a grand procession of parade floats occurs. The hoko is an elaborate float, which weighs 12 tons and is pulled on wheels that are as tall as people. This festival began in 869 and has never, once been stopped. It was originally held to appease the gods due to the smallpox outbreak and has been the longest consecutive festival ever known.

RESTAURANTS... CHARLIE'S CHOW TIME

Cuisine is a very integral part of Kyoto Prefecture and often rivals Tokyo.

BUDGET:

Asuka provides Teishoku meals. Eating an entire Teishoku meal is usually under **1,000 Yen**. One of their famed meals is Buri-ara netsuke teishoku, when in season. It is yellowtail simmered in a soy sauce with ginger. The side dishes include: rice, miso soup, vegetables, pickles, and tofu.

Toriyasu offers donburi, which is a rice bowl dish. The restaurant has served meals for 50 years, and is an offshoot of the 120-year-old restaurant next door. Both are worth checking out for meals between **600 and 800 Yen**. Kaage Donburi is one of the best meals, which is deep fried chicken, rice, and various toppings.

FANCY:

Hyotei is on the Nanzenji Temple grounds, where is has been since the 17th century. It is a family owned restaurant serving Japanese style cuisine. Kaiseki is the main meal, which starts at **23,000 Yen** for lunch and **27,000 Yen** for dinner. It is prepared with seasonal ingredients. The items are not as important as the preparation of the meal, which is designed to offer a color, appearance, taste and texture that will please the palate.

Nakamura is another historic restaurant dating to the 17th century. A three star Michelin restaurant it is also known for the seasonal items of the Kaiseki courses. At this location you will be sitting on Tatami mats. Prices begin at **20,000 Yen** including tax and increase from there.

NIGHTLIFE & ENTERTAINMENT... CHARLIE'S PARTY TIME

While Osaka is more popular for nightlife, Kyoto does have plenty of clubs and bars that accept foreign nationals. Many can be found in the Sanjo area close to Kawaramachi. A Bar is recommended for its pub and restaurant, as well as relaxing atmosphere. Ishimaru Shoten might be a little hard to find down an alley, but it offers a nice place to drink and enjoy music. Club Metro and Club World are the top two biggest clubs for music, dancing, and local acts.

LODGING... CHARLIE CHILL TIME

There are plenty of lodging options in Kyoto to make you content, whether you have a small or big budget.

BUDGET:

Budget Inn is a Ryokan style hostel for backpackers. It is a modest inn with private rooms and free Wi-Fi. It is set in a modern building with balconies for many of the rooms. Expect the cost to be **7,700+ Yen** plus a night.

Hotel Alpha Kyoto is in the Sanjo area of Kyoto. It offers comfortable amenities, a nearby convenience store, and friendly, educated staff. Based on the season you can expect to pay **8,300+ Yen** and up per night.

FANCY:

Mitsui Garden Hotel Kyoto Sanjo offers free Wi-Fi, an elegant hotel and plenty of amenities. At this hotel expect a spa, hot tub, garden, and tour options. As a popular hotel for travelers, expect the price to be **44,500 Yen** during the height of the season, per night.

Hotel Grande Minami is slightly more affordable, with less amenities at **22,200 Yen** per night. It does offer Wi-Fi, a car park, and is best for those seeking comfort. A nicety is offering breakfast served in your room, without an extra cost.

HIDDEN GEMS... CHARLIE'S TOP NON-TOURIST SITES

Taizo is just one of many temples in Kyoto, and often overlooked. It is the oldest of the Buddhist monastery complex, with stunning stone and sand landscape gardens, ceremonial tea, and a historic ink painting called the "Gourd and Catfish."

Kozan-ji is located close to the Tagano-o hamlet. It is a wooden temple that sits in an ancient forest on the slopes of Mount Takao in northwest Kyoto. It dates to 774 and became a Buddhist temple in 1206.

CITY 3: OSAKA

CHARLIE'S QUICK INTRO AND HISTORY

Osaka has a population of 2.5 million people, making it the third largest, yet second most important city in Japan. It has continued to excel in economic advancements for centuries, putting the Kansai region on the map for many businesses. Historically, Osaka was first called Naniwa. It was also the first capital city. As soon as a new emperor came into power the capital was moved. All of this happened before the Nara period. Toyotomi Hideyoshi chose Osaka, in the 16th century, to build his castle and had Tokugawa Ieyasu not ended the Toyotomi line with Hideyoshi's death, the city may once again been the capital.

CHARLIE'S FAVORITE TOUR SIGHTS & ADVENTURES

Sights Categories: Cultural, Historical Sites, Museums

1. Osaka Castle is a reconstruction of Hideyoshi's castle. It was destroyed by Oda Nobunaga 13 years after it was built and again destroyed by lightening in 1665. A Ferro-concrete construction was built to replicate the once splendorous castle to showcase important history. It also contains a museum.
2. Sumiyoshi Taisha is a shrine and one of the oldest in Japan. It was founded in the 3rd century as a place to instruct the Japanese on Buddhism. It is also a representative of Sumiyoshi-Zukuri architecture.

Adventure Categories: Urban, Outdoors, & Nature Activities

1. Universal Studios is the most popular theme park in the Kansai region.
2. Osaka Aquarium is considered one of the best in Japan, showcasing regional, national, and international marine species.

SHOPPING

Shopping is best in Umeda and Namba districts of Osaka. Umeda or Kita has several department stores, underground malls, and shopping arcades. Shinsaibashi Suji is one of the oldest malls and busiest destinations, with brand name stores, chain stores, boutiques, and several restaurants. Amerikamura is best for youth fashion, with inexpensive boutiques.

FESTIVALS

Osaka's most famous festival is Tenjin. The festival was started in the 10th century and is held in July each year. A parade procession occurs, with a river procession on the second day with fireworks. The festival honors Sugawara Michizan, a deity of scholarship. It is hosted at Tenmangu Shrine, which was important to the deity. The festival includes: food, local music, and costumes. There are some smaller festivals, but often the larger Kyoto based festivals outshine Osaka's.

RESTAURANTS… CHARLIE'S CHOW TIME

Osaka is often in a contest of better cuisine with Tokyo. Both cities can serve similar food, but prepared in totally different ways, making it worthwhile to test various places.

BUDGET:

Kougaryu is one of hundreds of takoyaki or meat on a stick stands in Japan. However, it is one of the highest rated in television shows, magazines and other media, as well as personally enjoyed. The prices are **330-550 Yen** per meal. Takoyaki can be chicken or other meats on a stick, usually fried and dipped in various sauces.

All-You-Can-Eat Yakinku might sound high at **1,100 Yen**, but it is a restaurant that lets you eat as much as you wish of the Yakiniku and shabu-shabu dishes. Yakiniku is literally grilled meat, where you are given a grill, a type of meat and side dishes to enjoy. The meat is tender and delicious at this restaurant. Shabu-shabu is sliced beef boiled in water, prepared with various vegetable side dishes.

FANCY:

Fujiya 1935 was opened in 2003 by Tetsuya Fujiwara, who trained in Spain and Italy. A well-known meal is Spaghettini of crab made with beans and mimoretto. A meal here is at least **20,000 Yen**.

Mizuno opened in 1945, right after World War II ended. It is the oldest Okonomiyaki restaurant in the city. Okonomiyaki is usually a flour based dough much like American pizza; however, Mizuno's uses a yam mixture, which is then loaded with various vegetables. Okonomiyaki is considered a Japanese pizza or pancake. Prices start at **6,000 Yen** and increase depending on ingredients and whether you order a full course meal.

NIGHTLIFE & ENTERTAINMENT... CHARLIE'S PARTY TIME

Osaka is known for its nightlife, particularly nightclubs like Giraffe. It is a place for dance and house music, as well as regular local events. Onzieme, which is also in the Shinsaibashi region is another location for music, drinks, and mingling. It is located on the 11th floor, so it is very easy to miss. Bar One is a wild weekend location, with plenty of music and a door fee of **1,000 to 2,000 Yen**. It is also near Giraffe and a fourth club called Club Pure. This club is known for hip hop, R&B, and plenty of free drinks. The drinks are actually covered in the door charge of **3,000 to 4,500 Yen** for guys and half that price for women.

LODGING... CHARLIE'S CHILL TIME

BUDGET:

First Cabin at Namba Station is a larger capsule hotel, where you can find a private room, which places it one step above a hostel. It is around **5,550 Yen** per night.

Boarding House at Tennoji Station offers private rooms, but shared showers. Still the convenience of location and a room to yourself makes it a great option for **2,780 Yen** per person, per night.

FANCY:

Hilton Osaka Hotel is for those who recognize the chain and want the poshest stay possible. Nights in high season are upwards of **55,600 Yen**, but worth the 20+ amenities, sauna, indoor pool, and fitness center.

Another option is the Swissotel Nakai Osaka, which offers a room for **44,500 Yen** plus a night during the busy season. Like the Hilton, expect a pool, private room, and plenty of amenities in a modern complex.

HIDDEN GEMS... CHARLIE'S TOP NON-TOURIST SITES

Osaka has many tourist attractions like Osaka Castle, Nipponbashi and Osaka Tower. What you will not find in most guide books is Namba Yasaka Shrine on any list. It is hidden near Namba Station in the heart of Osaka. It is an impressive location because of the giant lion heads coupled with a rich history dating to the 5th century. It is also a shrine that represents the Gonzu Tennou deity, who is believed to cure illnesses.

Shikitsumatsunomiya is an Okuninushi Shrine close to Daikokucho Station. The shrine was built for two deities: relating to business and medical concerns. At this shrine, visitors can learn the myths and tales about the Susanoo or the god of storms. The shrine was built in 1744. One of the more famous tales is about a hare that went about stealing goddesses' hearts in order to bring them to Susanoo for torture.

CITY 4: NARA

CHARLIE'S QUICK INTRO AND HISTORY

Nara was the first permanent capital city of Japan. It was established in 710, at what was then called Heijo. Buddhist monasteries start to rise in power, influencing the city and political frame of mind. For the safety of the Japanese government, it was decided to move the capital to Nagaoka in 784. Nara is approximately an hour from Kyoto and Osaka. Given its history as the first permanent capital, there are plenty of historic and national treasures, such as the oldest and largest of the Japanese temples.

CHARLIE'S FAVORITE TOUR SIGHTS & ADVENTURES

Sights Categories: Cultural, Historical Sites, Museums

1. Todaiji Temple is the largest in the area with a monumental Buddha statue to welcome you.
2. Horyuji Temple holds the distinction of being the world's oldest wooden building.
3. Toshodaiki Temple is a large temple in the western part of Nara city. It will remind you of the small, traditional Japanese houses, with gardens.

Adventure Categories: Urban, Outdoors, & Nature Activities

1. Isuien Garden is located near Todaiji. It contains several Japanese gardens with ponds and bridges.
2. Nara Park is known for wild deer sightings. It is also a place to picnic, take a walk, or watch sporting events.

3. Yoshikien Garden Houses Japanese style buildings, along with three distinct gardens.

FESTIVALS

Nara has several festivals relating to the old capital. However, the biggest and most interesting festival is held in January. It is called Wakakusa Yamayaki and an entire hillside of Mount Wakakusayama is set on fire. The mountain is on the eastern side of Nara Park. One theory is that the festival started to drive away wild boars during the feudal eras. Omizutori is another burning event. It happens at the Nigatsudo hall to celebrate the Buddhist repentance ritual, which has been ongoing for 1250 years. This festival is held in March.

RESTAURANTS… CHARLIE'S CHOW TIME

BUDGET:
Le Dimanche Boulangerie is a wonderful bakery for breakfast and sandwiches. The Viennese Cranberry roll is their most famous bread, which is a few hundred Yen.

Yanagi-Ji-Ya is a place to try warabi mocha for morning and afternoon tea. It is a bracken fern root, with soybean flour and brown sugar syrup. They also serve bentos, which are slightly more expensive at around **500 Yen**.

FANCY:

Akashiya serves grilled octopus and gyoza dumplings. Expect meals to begin around **20,000 Yen** for a full course, fixed meal price.

Harishin is known for the kamitsumichi bento box, which is offered at **2,900 Yen**. However, you can also enjoy a sit down meal overlooking the garden or hearth.

NIGHTLIFE & ENTERTAINMENT... CHARLIE'S PARTY TIME

Nara is more of a student city, meaning there are fewer locations for nightlife. Mainly walking in some of the parks, enjoying a drink at a bar, and going to the theater are the main attractions at night.

LODGING... CHARLIE CHILL TIME

BUDGET:

Hotel Fine Garden Nara Kashiba is a grand hotel for a budget. Rooms begin at **4,450 Yen** a night. Amenities are free Wi-Fi and private rooms.

Super Hotel Lohas JR Nara Station is slightly less budget friendly, but not as fancy as the Nara Hotel. You can stay here for **8,900 Yen** and up a night. A hot spring bath, free Wi-Fi and elevators make this hotel worth considering.

FANCY:

Nara Hotel is an amazing facility based on a Japanese temple. You definitely want to avoid Golden Week and any festival week to visit this hotel because the prices can be as high as **222,500 Yen** a night. It is of particular interest because it is a famous hotel built in 1909 and offers panoramic views of the city. It is like an authentic stay in an imperial palace.

HIDDEN GEMS… CHARLIE'S TOP NON-TOURIST SITES

On top of the **Nara Prefectural Office** is a magnificent view of the city and surrounding prefecture of Nara. Another amazing gem is located at **Ukimido Pavilion**, which is built over a beautiful lake. Going here can be relaxing.

CITY 5: OKINAWA

CHARLIE'S QUICK INTRO AND HISTORY

Okinawa is mostly known as the place for the US military base, established after the First World War. Yet, it is much more than that as a city and prefecture. Okinawa is the southernmost prefecture made up of several islands like the Nansei Shoto chain, which is a thousand kilometers in size. Okinawa can be divided into three major island groups: Okinawa Shoto, Yaeyama Retto and Miyako Retto. The temperate climate makes for a wonderful place for coral reefs, marine life, and thus scuba diving. Ryukyu Islands, which are part of Okinawa is a main attraction due to the Chinese history and culture that represents the islands past.

CHARLIE'S FAVORITE TOUR SIGHTS & ADVENTURES

Sights Categories: Cultural, Historical Sites, Museums

1. Churaumi Aquarium is the leading aquarium in the world with whale sharks.
2. War Memorials relating to Peace Park.
3. The Ocean Expo Park is another amusement park.
4. Shuri Castle is a reconstruction of the former Ryukyu Royal Palace.

Adventure Categories: Urban, Outdoors, & Nature Activities

1. Sefa Utaki is a sacred site on Okinawa Island. It is indigenous to Okinawan religion, which is related to Shinto. Nature and the worship of it is the main focus at this site.

2. Hiji Waterfall near Yambaru is a natural forest, which sustained some damage in 2012, but is now open with newly constructed trails and an amazing suspension bridge to the 26-meter-tall waterfall.
3. Shikinaen is a residence, but also known for the Japanese landscape gardens with a central pond.
4. Okinawa World is both a historical site and one of nature, with its natural caves alongside the ocean.

SHOPPING

Shopping is possible in four locations. Chindami Sanshinten, Kosetsu Ichiba Market, Tsuboya Pottery District, and Yachimun no Sato Pottery Village are the best places to shop for tourists. Chindami Sanshinten is a mall, which will also be a place to hear authentic sanshin music. The market is more of an arcade of shops from tourist locations to boutiques. The two pottery locations are places to get ancient pottery or to see how 300 years of pottery making has become more modern.

FESTIVALS

Okinawa is home to the International Movie Festival. It is a weeklong adventure, which is in its eighth year. Okinawa is also the city for Naha Dragon Boat races, which is part of a festival in June. There are also the Star Festival and Sea Day. Okinawa also hosts a Festival of Souls, which is in August and lasts for two days.

RESTAURANTS… CHARLIE'S CHOW TIME

BUDGET:

Chuzan is a tavern with goya champuru (stir-fry with bitter melon) and Korean bibimbap. Prices are extremely affordable starting around **300 Yen**.

Goya offers a place of rustic charm with wooden walls, and alcoves full of dolls and farm implements. They are known for their awamori rice liquor and rafute bacon with soy sauce, ginger root, and brown sugar. Here you can enjoy drinks and a meal starting at **500 Yen**.

FANCY:

Hateruma is a lively location and considered an Izakaya style restaurant with music and dance shows. Expect Goya Champloo meal sets, which start at **860 Yen**.

Mafali Café is near Makishi Station and considered an eclectic location. They offer everything from tacos, curry soup to alligator steaks, coffee and cake sets. Meals begin around **1,000 Yen** and increase depending on the time of day.

NIGHTLIFE & ENTERTAINMENT... CHARLIE'S PARTY TIME

Okinawa is known for its nightlife that caters to US military personnel. Expect plenty of bars, pubs, and dance clubs like **Bar Alchemist, Dojo Bar and South Park**. All are great hangouts for getting affordable drinks and entertainment.

LODGING... CHARLIE CHILL TIME

BUDGET:

Hyper Hotel Ishigaki offers all the amenities you would want in a western style hotel for a budget. You can expect prices to begin around **6,600 Yen** per night depending on the season. There is a range of rooms for families as well as couples.

Lue on the Beach is 20 minutes from the main attractions in Okinawa. It is a bungalow style hotel with a restaurant, beach, and Spartan rooms. However, the budget fits with rooms starting at **5,500 Yen** depending on the season.

FANCY:

Hotel Royal Orion is just north of the Makishi monorail. Rooms begin at **7,700 Yen** per night and increase based on size and season. This hotel offers nicely furnished rooms, with all the amenities you need for your comfort.

Busena Terrace has a great location, luxury furnishings and top of the line facilities, including a spa. US Presidents and millionaires have stayed here. Prices are usually upwards of **33,500 Yen** a night for regular rooms.

HIDDEN GEMS... CHARLIE'S TOP NON-TOURIST SITES

Kajinhou is an older Okinawan style house, which offers amazing views. It is also a restaurant, run by second generation family members. This Kensaku location has run for 100 years and will continue to be a warm and welcoming place. Another amazing restaurant that is also a hidden gem is located in **Gangala Valley**, a natural park with plenty of caves. One of those caves includes a café with amazing coffee and a very photographic location with stalactites and stalagmites for company.

CITY 6: HOKKAIDO

CHARLIE'S QUICK INTRO AND HISTORY

Hokkaido is considered the second largest of the four main Japan islands. It is also the northernmost grouping. It is known for its extremely cold temperatures, where the seas can freeze and temperatures can reach below zero. Nature is relatively unscathed here, even from skiers and snowboarders who frequent in the winter seasons. History dates the first mention in 720 AD. A text called Abe No Hirafu stated navy and army used the island in 658 to 660. The Ainu people inhabited the land, according to early Japanese texts. It was not until the Muromachi period when people began to leave the southern areas due to increased battles that issues occurred between the traded goods coming from the north to the south. Several disputes started between Japanese and Ainu people, leading to a war where Takeda Nobuhiro killed the Ainu leader. Nobuhiro ancestors ruled the area until the end of the Edo period. There was a worry that the Russians would invade the northern island and take control of Hokkaido prefecture; however, it was only a temporary worry, with the Meiji Government gaining control during the Boshin War.

Hokkaido is a prefecture with several cities, including Niseko, Furano, Sapporo, Hakodate, Noboribetsu, and Otaru.

CHARLIE'S FAVORITE TOUR SIGHTS & ADVENTURES

Plenty awaits any visitor to this region, which is full of various cities and resort towns.

Sights Categories: Cultural, Historical Sites, Museums

1. Hokkaido Museum is a place of history, nature and cultural exhibits.
2. Hokkaido Museum of Modern Art is filled with contemporary art and glass art.
3. Usakumai is a national historic site in Chitose.
4. Otafunbe Chashi is in Urahoro and named for the world whale.

Adventure Categories: Urban, Outdoors, & Nature Activities

1. Rusutsu offers skiing.
2. Noboribetsu is a hot spring resort.
3. Jozankei Onsen is another hot spring resort, although second largest in size.
4. Asahikawa is known for the zoo and aquarium.
5. Shiretoko is a national park that is untouched in its beauty.
6. Daisetsuzan is the largest national park and home to most of Japan's wildlife.

SHOPPING

The best place to shop is at the "village" outlet, which is located near the New Chitose Airport. It offers the best items that you would find in department stores.

FESTIVALS

Hokkaido is known for three festivals: Sapporo Snow Festival, Asahikawa Winter Festival and Otaru Snow Light Path. These festivals are held in the winter months to honor the tourist season. Without the snow, which allows skiing many areas in Hokkaido would be sleepy little towns.

RESTAURANTS… CHARLIE'S CHOW TIME

Restaurants in Hokkaido are mostly located in Sapporo, but there are a couple in Otaru and Niseko. A lot of the cities have restaurants attached to hotels, which make them a little fancier.

BUDGET:

Bangaichi Café is a small, windowless location, which is above the main street in Abashiri. The menu is known for its hemp and raisin scores and cheese on toast. Most items are around **300 Yen**.

Zazi is a coffee shop with an English menu. Eats here are **1,000 Yen** for a power lunch, which includes two fried eggs, sausage, salad, potatoes, and bread.

FANCY:

Daruma is a 45-year-old location known for its lamb jingisukan. Plates start at **700 Yen** and increase.

Izakaya Bang offers Yakitori, but at a fancier location with seating. It is located in Hirafu Village and generally around **500 Yen** and up for meals.

NIGHTLIFE & ENTERTAINMENT... CHARLIE'S PARTY TIME

Nightlife in Hokkaido cities is all about bars and restaurants. Many people come off the slopes to get a meal, warm up, and a little drink before preparing for the next day of skiing fun.

LODGING... CHARLIE CHILL TIME

BUDGET:

Hotel Maki is run by the Inada family. They offer a nice quiet place to stay for skiing and other Hokkaido attractions. They offer a stay that is budget friendly; however, rates are not available as they are subject to seasonal changes. It is known that breakfast is **870 Yen**.

Lakeside Spa Toya Kawanami is another family owned location for a budget, which is also based on the season. It is an easy walk to dinner, the village, and shoreline.

FANCY:

Authent Hotel is more of an upscale, elegant hotel, which is about a mid-range price. Prices are not available unless looking for specific dates, but you can expect **11,100+ Yen** a night.

Grand Park Otaru is located at the marina with an 18 story hotel sitting on top of the WingBay shopping complex. Prices are nearer to **22,500 Yen** or more a night depending on the season.

HIDDEN GEMS... CHARLIE'S TOP NON-TOURIST SITES

Sounkyo Gorge is often forgotten in place of skiing and closer parks to the major cities. However, if visiting Daisetsuzan National Park then you will want to make sure to see the Sounkyo Gorge.

CITY 7: HIROSHIMA

CHARLIE'S QUICK INTRO AND HISTORY

Hiroshima became the world's stage when the atomic bomb was dropped there in 1945. It was the first time in history that such a powerful weapon was used on any country, where everything within 2 kilometers was wiped out. For a time, it was thought the destructive bomb would make the city uninhabitable, but eventually the dust cleared and it was safe to return. Today, the numerous heritage sites destroyed in the bombing have been reconstructed like Hiroshima Castle and Shukkeien Garden. A large park was built in memory of those who lost their lives and the park is aptly named Peace Memorial Park.

Prior to the destructive bomb, Hiroshima was a powerful sea location, under the rule of Mori Terumoto. He reigned from 1589 until his death. He lost in battles against Tokugawa Ieyasu. During the imperial period, the area became an urban center, with important industries, and schools. It reached importance as a port city in the 1880s. It also housed the military transportation for the First Sino-Japanese War. It was also very militarized for the First and Second World Wars. The Army Marine headquarters were located at Ujina port, and key military supplies were kept there. This is why the US targeted it after the destruction of Hawaii's Pearl Harbor. However, the casualty list was much larger than just military personnel due to radiation.

CHARLIE'S FAVORITE TOUR SIGHTS & ADVENTURES

Sights Categories: Cultural, Historical Sites, Museums

1. Peace Park is the memorial and park created to remember the atomic bombing in 1945. Visitors can learn about the damaging effects the bomb caused and the Japanese view of the destructive actions the US took.
2. Mazda Museum is all about the local car maker, the factory tour, and the museum of Mazda models that have been built.
3. Hiroshima Downtown is a great place to see how the city has returned after the bombing, as well as to see the culture of today in the malls, restaurants, and buildings.
4. Hiroshima Castle is a reconstruction of the one built by Terumoto in the 1500s.

Adventure Categories: Urban, Outdoors, & Nature Activities

1. Shukkeien Garden literally meaning Shrunken Scenery Garden. It is a mixture of valleys, mountains, and forests represented by miniature landscapes. It is also a part of Hiroshima Castle. There are traditional Japanese Gardens, tea houses, and plenty of ponds to walk around.
2. Iwakuni is a small side trip from the city center, in the prefecture, where one can walk, enjoy the cherry blossoms and the Kintai-kyo Bridge.

SHOPPING

Hiroshima's downtown is where all the shops and indoor malls are located. Simply going downtown can bring visitors to any number of big Japanese department store chains, boutiques, and food courts.

FESTIVALS

Residents of Hiroshima spend a day to remember the bombing in 1945. While, there is no official festival, there are often events and surviving family members who visit the memorials of loved ones. There is also a cherry blossom location called Hanami Spots, where many come to view the cherry blossoms when in full bloom.

RESTAURANTS... CHARLIE'S CHOW TIME

Hiroshima is known for its okonomiyaki, oysters, momijimanju, and tsukemen cold noodles. Most of the dining locations are in downtown Hiroshima and close to Hiroshima Station.

BUDGET:

Onigiri Nitaya offers bentos for those who wish to take a picnic lunch, while visiting the sites. Affordable at **300 Yen** and up, it is a great place to get a meal with side dishes to take on your travels for the day.

Zona Bel Pizza is a hilltop restaurant, with Italian pizza. Many of the dishes begin at **380 Yen** like the Poca Mozeralla Pizza or Marinara based pizza.

FANCY:

Yakigaki-no-hayashi is known for its barbecue and raw oysters. They offer bento boxes too, with many of the meals starting around **900 Yen**. At this restaurant you can enjoy an authentic Japanese experience or take your bento box to go.

Okonomi-mura is considered the best place in Hiroshima to get okonomiyaki. Although, not as fancy as you would find in Osaka or Tokyo, this restaurant offers great food starting around **500 Yen**.

NIGHTLIFE & ENTERTAINMENT... CHARLIE'S PARTY TIME

Hiroshima does have a few bars in the hotels and Hiroshima Nagarekawa is considered a place to go for music, girls, and drinks. More of a business city, Hiroshima caters to business people with bars and restaurants.

LODGING... CHARLIE CHILL TIME

BUDGET:

Hotel Livemax Mihara-ekimae is more for the budget, with free cancellation, private rooms, and views of the city. It is

5,200 Yen per night and up. There is a bar, daily housekeeping and free Wi-Fi.

Hotel Areaone Hiroshimawing is another place with free cancellation, private rooms, and comfortable beds. Rates start at **6,300 Yen** per night. There is a bar, free Wi-Fi and daily housekeeping among the amenities.

FANCY:

Hotel Granvia Hiroshima offers 403 rooms, a business center, Wi-Fi, coffee shop, restaurant, and bar. It is one of the nicer hotels in the area with peak pricing at $180 to $250 per night.

Chisun Hotel Hiroshima is not as fancy as the Granvia; however, it does offer a spa, massage, business facilities and bike rental all for **7,700 to 9,900 Yen** during the peak season. It is a newer hotel located in the center of town.

HIDDEN GEMS… CHARLIE'S TOP NON-TOURIST SITES

If you have time, you will want to stop by the **Memorial Tower to the Mobilized Students**. It is a difficult place to go and not always on the most visited lists because it commemorates 6,300 students who were conscripted to work in the munitions factories destroyed by the bomb.

The Rest House is run by a survivor, an employee who worked for the Taishoya Kimono Shop that was bombed. The survivor turned the area into a gift shop, tourist location, and a place to rest.

CHARLIE'S FAREWELL NOTE

We hope you have enjoyed the journey with Charlie and can head back home with plenty of stories for friends and family! We urge you to take this time to reflect on all that you have learned and witnessed over the last couple of days. These are the experiences that last forever and we cannot thank you enough for choosing us as your travel companion. We, the Unbound Charlie team, are forever grateful for choosing us as your preferred travel guide!

Our Unbound Charlie team takes the utmost pride in satisfying our travelers. If you enjoyed the journey with us, please don't forget to rate and leave us a review so that others may travel with Charlie as well!

We wish you safe future travels.

Warm regards,
Unbound Charlie

Made in the USA
Lexington, KY
07 November 2016